What the successful teach their children

ALPHABET FOR SUCCESS
2nd Edition 2015

Copyright © 2013 Francine K Woolcock

All rights reserved.

ISBN: 1494738104
ISBN-13: 978-1494738105

DEDICATION

I dedicate this book to my grandmother Clovis Plummer for standing by me in all my endeavours. Most of all, for bringing me breakfast, lunch and dinner during the hours I spent dedicated to the completion of this book.
Love you Nan x

CONTENTS

Acknowledgments	i
Preface	1
How to use this book	3
Affirm	4
Bold	7
Confidence	9
Desire	11
Effort	14
Focus	17
Goal	19
Health	21
Initiative	24
Joy	27
Knowledge	30
Love	33
Motivation	35
Nearest & Dearest	38
Optimism	40
Positivity	42
Question	45

Resilience	48
Strong-minded	51
Thankful	54
Unwavering	56
Visualization	58
Willpower	60
Xenodochial	62
Youth	64
Zest	67

ACKNOWLEDGMENTS

I would like to express my greatest appreciation to God for giving me life.

I would like to thank all the sources used that have provided me with information with which to support the messages conveyed in this book. These sources have been referenced toward the closing of this book.

PREFACE

It is important to note that this is a parental guide and therefore, written for you as an aid to guide your protégé.

This is an alphabet like no other.
In this book, each letter of the alphabet highlights an attribute that, if applied, has a positive effect on your child's ability to succeed in anything they do.
These 26 words, their meanings and their importance are practiced by many entrepreneurs, leaders and anyone who has ever achieved anything in their life.

Guidance has been provided in the form of games and instructions to encourage interaction and to help make the learning process fun and engaging for the child.

******

At the time of writing this book, I was surprised to find that, although there were many resources including guides to promote success and a positive mental attitude in adults, the marketplace for resources teaching children the same principles were somewhat limited.

Knowing that most habits portrayed by adults are formed during the earlier stages of development and remain in your subconscious mind affecting your beliefs and actions (a topic that requires a much greater coverage than I am able to provide in this book and give respect to what is a detailed and important subject), it is imperative that these principles are taught to our children now, in the earlier stages of life.

The most common feedback I get from teaching these attributes to many of my adult friends is, 'I know this now, but I wish my parents had pulled me up and guided me to think like this when I was younger, I would have achieved';-then they list all the things they had wanted to do when they were younger, all the things they regretted not trying because they lacked strength in one or more of these attributes.

This book should be kept close and used as a reference as and when you believe that one of these attributes requires strengthening.

HOW TO USE THIS BOOK

- ✓ Each Letter of the alphabet, depicts one attribute of a successful individual.
- ✓ Follow the simple steps to introduce and or maintain each characteristic.
- ✓ Activities are to be carried out at your child's pace with your guidance.
- ✓ Repeat the 'positive words for your child', to your child frequently to build a success mentality.

Bonus: Many Attributes are closely linked, therefore, practicing one, may automatically lead to the strengthening of another.

REMEMBER:

'It is not what you do for your children, but what you have taught them to do for themselves, that will make them successful human beings'. – Esther Pauline Lederer

..........(Better known as Ann Landers (pen name), an American advice columnist who was recognized in a 1978 World Almanac survey as the most influential woman in the United States.

Disclaimer:
This book contains some universal laws that, although have not all been proven by science, have been accepted by great leaders and successful individuals.

Some exercises may be supported by the research and studies of child psychology, however, this is not the rule and some are based on evidence from experience. Reference to papers and studies have been cited where required.

Francine K Woolcock

Affirm

Affirm:-
A statement of the existence or truth of something

Ever had someone tell you something that, initially you may not have believed, but they tell you over and over and over again until one day, you find yourself believing.

When you affirm something, you declare it to be true.
Even if there is no logic behind a statement, quite often, if enough people say it, enough times, one day, belief will soon follow.

Children are learning from what you and others tell them, show them, and do. Do not affirm negative ideas.

Popularized by great teachers of positive thinking and success such as Napoleon Hill, Tony Robbins, Rhonda Byrne and many others. It is thought that the affirming statements themselves, lead to subsequent physical actions as we automatically will do things to support our beliefs.

In-order for affirmations to be effective, they must be in the presentence and be personal.

Positive affirmations only- Positive affirmations daily

1) Encourage positive self affirmations and discourage negative ones.

   - ✓ I FEEL GREAT
   - ✓ I CAN DO IT

- ✓ I AM HAPPY
- ✓ I FEEL TERRIFIC
- ✓ I AM GOOD AT…

2) Affirmations must be stated in the positive. Not 'I will', but, 'I am'.

Positive Words for your child

"Whether you think that you can, or that you can't, you are usually right." Henry Ford

What the successful teach their children –Alphabet for Success

Bold

Bold:-
Courageous, confident, and fearless; ready to take risks

HOW TO ENCOURAGE A BOLD ATTITUDE

Alleviate fears

Many children are reserved / shy because they are afraid of the outcome of their actions. Advise your child that it is ok to make mistakes. Never embarrass, scold or criticize your child's mistakes. Instead, correct them by offering guidance on how to do things correctly next time. Mistakes are expected due to your child's lack of experience.

Trying new things

Where possible, introduce your child to different activities and experiences. This will help them to develop new skills and make a habit of trying new things.

Protect, but don't overprotect

As parents, there is a natural instinct to protect your child from taking risks that may be harmful; however, there is a thin line between being protective and overprotecting. Try not to stunt your child's development and self-improvement by preventing them from taking beneficial, safe risks.

Positive Words for your child

"You'll never know unless you try." unknown

What the successful teach their children –Alphabet for Success

Confidence

Confidence:-
Belief in one's own abilities

YES YOU CAN

The old saying 'There's no such word as can't ', is still relevant. Convince your child they CAN at all times and provide assistance to help achieve their goal.

Reasons for a lack of Confidence and how to deal with it

- Lack of knowledge – Increase studying in that area.
- Fear of failure – Change their way of thinking, there is no such thing as failure, instead, they have succeeded at finding one way how 'not' to do something and are now closer to achieving their goal.
- Lack of experience- Repeat the task until your child is comfortable. The actual task could be repeated, but also, do not underestimate role play, aka pretend play that children will often engage in. This is a very powerful tool.

Positive Words for your child

"What the mind of man can conceive and believe, it can achieve." Napoleon Hill

What the successful teach their children –Alphabet for Success

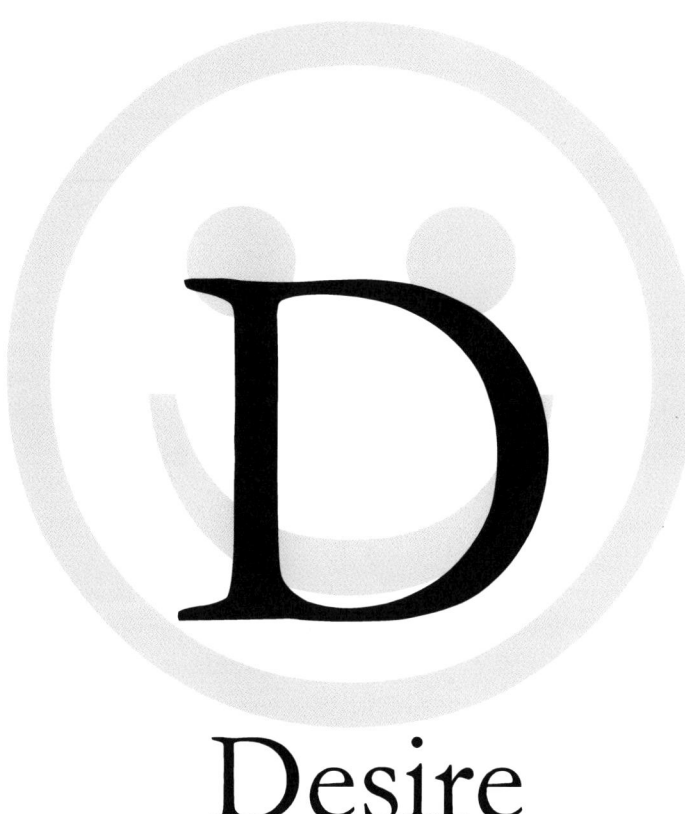

Desire

Desire:-
To express a wish or make a request for

Having a desire is the backbone to success

Did you know, the more you think about something, the more likely you are to get it?

Simplifying the Science:
Having a desire for something increases the dopamine levels in the brain. (Dopamine is a neurotransmitter which is a chemical that transmits signals between the nerve cells (neurons) of the brain).
Increased dopamine levels enables the prefrontal cortex (part of the brain responsible for processing complex thought and goals, amongst other things) to focus more clearly, increases the number of connections the brain can make per second and helps learners to hold on to new ideas.

<u>Maintain your child's desire:</u>
Keep their eyes on the reward by consistently asking you child 'what' they want, and 'why' do they want what they want. By answering this question, your child will reaffirm their desire.
Importantly, if your child has no desires then, they will be easily influenced by others and what others want to do and may fail to attract their own success.

Creating desire:

A desire, if not already present, can be borne by encouraging the creation of goals (see G for Goals).

Positive Words for your child

"Whatever you desire, you will achieve, whether it's something, or nothing." Francine Woolcock

Francine K Woolcock

Effort

Effort:-
A determined (unwavering) attempt

YOU GET WHAT YOU PUT IN

From an early age, teach your child that nothing comes freely, or by luck. Results and luxuries are a direct result of how much effort you make.

Work Smarter, not Harder
It is a common misconception that more effort means physically working harder. As humans, our maximum brain potential greatly outweighs our physical potential. Therefore, it is important to spend a greater deal of time mentally analyzing a task than it is physically trying to work on a task.

IMPORTANT: Always reward and praise children according to their efforts rather than focusing on the end results.

Play the challenge game; recommended at least once a month.

Depending on your child's ability, give them something to do which you know will be a challenge, but achievable with some effort, and review their success.

You will find that new skills are developed in the process and the challenges will become easier to achieve. Continue to push their boundaries and do not allow them to give-up.

Positive Words for your child

"..If at first you don't succeed, try, try again" the writings of Thomas H. Palmer

What the successful teach their children –Alphabet for Success

Focus

Focus:-
A point upon which attention, activity, etc, is directed or concentrated

HOW TO KEEP YOUR CHILD FOCUSED

With our hectic lifestyles, media and social distractions, it is difficult for anyone to remain focused, let-alone a curious child. For children, life is new and exciting, most are not yet focused, which is expected as they try to find themselves, their likes and dislikes.

One way to keep our children Focused?

One thing at a time

Often we regard 'multi-tasking' as a skill, however, task management which reduces the need to multi-task is a much more efficient way of working.

As soon as you get a hint of loss of interest, whether it be, studying, homework or even playing games or eating; unless there is a valid reason to change focus mid-completion, nip it in the bud early and encourage the habit of completing one thing before beginning another. Remind the child why they started the activity in the first place and redirect their interest.

Positive Words for your child

"Just like a camera lens, if you lose your focus then your vision is blurred. If you refuse to sharpen your focus, then expect poor results." Francine Woolcock

What the successful teach their children –Alphabet for Success

Goal

Goal:-

The terminal point of a journey or race

IS THERE A PLAN?

Many people do not succeed because they have not defined any goals to base their success on.
A goal gives children a sense of direction and an aim in life.

Sit down with your child and write down their goals:-
For short term (immediately- 1year) and long term (anything after a year). N.b. these time frames are geared at children, as adults generally consider long term to be anything over 5 years.

Once goals are set, it is important to then, make a list of things that need to be done to achieve the goals. These are called objectives.
Important: Ensure the goals set are decided by your child with little influence from yourself so they feel in control.

GOAL + ACTION + ATTRIBUTE = SUCCESS

Positive Words for your child

If you don't set any goals, you don't have a plan.

"He, who fails to plan, plans to fail." Winston Churchill

What the successful teach their children –Alphabet for Success

Health:-
The general condition of body and mind

Without good health, it would be impossible to succeed.
For the purposes of this book, good health is not determined by your physical abilities / disabilities. Good Health in this instance is defined as providing your mind, body and soul with the fuel it needs to operate at its optimal state.

Mind – Condition the mind to think positively and successfully.
- Take care of the words used around, toward and by your child. Encourage positivity and discourage negativity.
- Control the media that influences your child, so far as is reasonable practicable, i.e. controlling the television programs watched, and encourage as much non-fiction, self-help, educational viewing, literature and audio as possible.

Body – Every cell in the body requires specific nutrients to function correctly. Treat food as fuel rather than just a means to satisfy hunger.
- There are thousands of books to assist in the correct diet for optimal performance. Feed your children a healthy diet. This does not have to be costly if a degree of planning is carried out.
Garbage in = Garbage out.

Soul - There are many descriptions of what the soul is. In this instance, the soul refers to the silent guide within you.
The soul is responsible for the psychic type feelings we have called intuition and hunches, our déjà vu experiences and our compassion

toward strangers in adversity.
- Feed the soul by teaching your child love and specifically philanthropy (the love of humanity).

Positive Words for your child

"Your body is like a car, everything is in tip top condition when you first get it, it gets mileage with time, but no servicing and the wrong fuel will cause it to breakdown."
Francine Woolcock

Francine K Woolcock

Initiative

Initiative:-
The first step or action on a matter

When we are born, our body kicks into action to function to survive, this is seen when we take our first breath. Nobody takes this for us, neither our friends nor family. This initiative is carried out by our subconscious because science proves that at birth we cannot yet consciously make that decision.

So why do we, as we grow older, **consciously** become dependent on others to take initiatives?

> Everything that we do and don't do, no-matter how big or small, will shape our future.
>
> We must take control.

Ever catch yourself saying- 'but why have I got to tell you do that?!' Probably because you keep telling them to do that.

REASONS WHY THE INITIATIVE IS SOMETIMES NOT TAKEN

Responsibility
Quite often, the failure to take the initiative is due to a lack of ownership. The first step is not taken because we leave the responsibility of the task to someone else. Reasonable

responsibilities should be given to children, such as tidying their room. However, the main message, should be that, 'your achievement and success depends on your own actions'.

Procrastination

So many of us play the 'I want to...., but' card. We procrastinate and seldom take action which often leads to regret and missed opportunities.

Treating every day as the same

Every day is not alike, the opportunities and conditions today will change in some way tomorrow.

Positive Words for your child

"Some people want it to happen, Some people Wish it would happen, others MAKE it happen." Michael Jordan

What the successful teach their children –Alphabet for Success

Joy:-

A deep feeling or condition of happiness or contentment

SCIENCE PROVES HAPPY PEOPLE ARE MORE SUCCESSFUL

The link between happiness and success was investigated by a team from the University of California Riverside, led by Professor Sonja Lyubomirsky.

'When people feel happy, they tend to feel confident, optimistic, and energetic and others find them likable and sociable.'

Smiling releases the chemicals called endorphins which automatically make you feel good.

HOW TO BE HAPPIER- TEACH CHILDREN THE FOLLOWING:

Be grateful.
People have reported happiness that lasted for weeks and months after writing letters of gratitude to others (they don't even have to be sent), or just make a list of all that you are grateful for.
Be optimistic.
Visualizing positive circumstances and outcomes increases happiness.
Count your blessings.
Write three positive things that happen each week.

Use your strengths.
Identify strengths and make a commitment to try to use them in new ways.

Act kindly.
People who help others report that it also helps their own sense of well-being.

Positive Words for your child

"You'll know if you've succeeded if you can't stop smiling, and if you stop smiling, you'll no-longer succeed."
Francine Woolcock

GUIDE → ENCOURAGE → REWARD

Francine K Woolcock

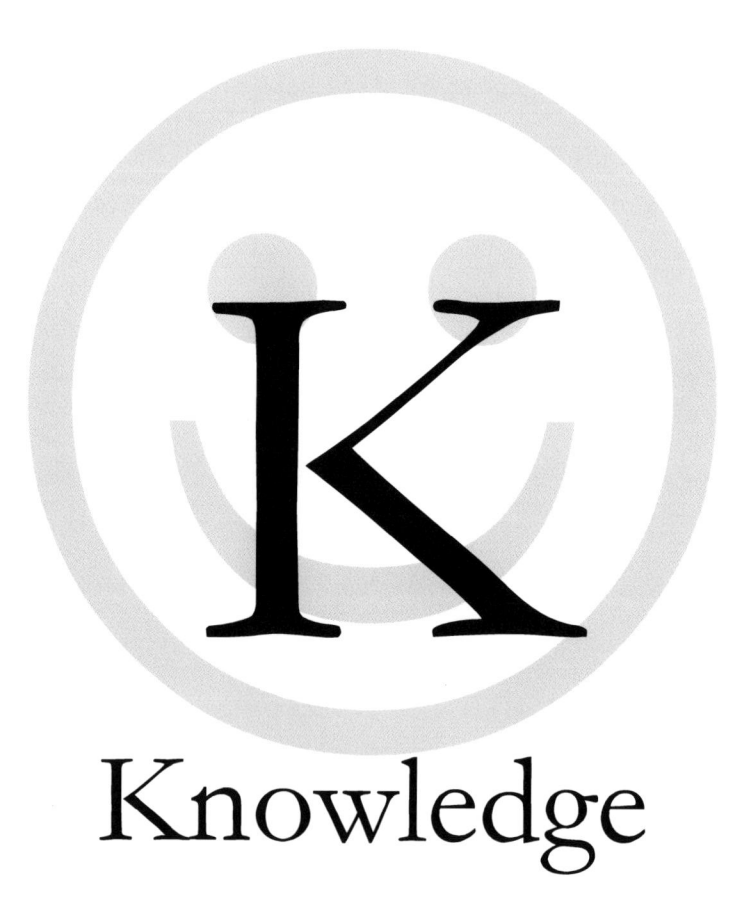

K

Knowledge

Knowledge:-
The state of knowing

Knowledge- available and vast

"There is nothing new under the sun". "Everything new has already been done". We hear these phrases all the time. Therefore, we can confidently say, there is a world of knowledge available to us.
So many people try to re-invent the wheel, but the successful have grasped the concept of using available knowledge and know that a little research saves, time & money.

Cultivate Seekers & Individuals who know when they don't know.
A terrible attitude that stifles growth and success, is believing that you know it all.

As adults we develop a terrible feeling called 'embarrassment'. What this does is prevents us from admitting our weaknesses and keeps us in a state of not knowing as we are too embarrassed to admit our lack of knowledge.

Children begin life with an inquisitive mind, seeking knowledge in a world that is new to them. It is important that they are encouraged to continue to do this.

SOME THINGS THAT CHILDREN CAN DO TO INCREASE THEIR KNOWLEDGE ...

Read more educational material	Ask questions
Use the Internet more frequently for research rather than leisure	Join an after school club.
Museum trips	Socialize

Positive Words for your child

"Knowledge is power" Francis Bacon

GUIDE ➤ ENCOURAGE ➤ REWARD

What the successful teach their children –Alphabet for Success

L

Love

Love:-
An intense emotion of affection, warmth, fondness, and regard towards a person or thing

Love yourself
Lesson one is to love yourself by thinking only positive thoughts about yourself; not to be confused with vanity which is to overindulge in ones appearance and abilities.

Love others
They that love are in a better position to be successful because it is well known that what you give is what you shall receive. Give more love and receive more love.

THE SIMPLEST WAY TO ENCOURAGE YOUR CHILD TO BE MORE LOVING IS TO GIVE YOUR CHILD MORE LOVE.

Positive Words for your child

"If I love what I do, then I'll succeed even quicker."
Francine Woolcock

GUIDE → ENCOURAGE → REWARD

What the successful teach their children –Alphabet for Success

M

Motivation

Motivation:-
Desire to do; interest or drive

MOTIVATION FOR SUCCESS

Motivation is always present, as the desire to do something is always present. The key is to remain motivated toward your ambition / plan, i.e., choosing to watch T.V instead of doing homework.

MOTIVATING CHILDREN

Do not steal control
As explained under G for Goals, It is important to allow your child to set their own goals and desires, doing this, will allow the child to feel in-control.
Children generally will become disinterested in a task if they feel they no longer are in control.
To regain control, they will oppose the requests of the force they feel to have taken over control.

Teach Responsibility and consequences
In some instances, a child may become de-motivated through sheer laziness.
If a child becomes de-motivated and decides to quit something before completing /contribute less effort, they should be made aware of the consequences in doing so.

    For example, if at first, a child is extremely motivated to join a football team and then becomes lazy and no longer wishes to practice, do not force them to go to practice in an effort to motivate them because they will not commit their full efforts.
Instead, warn them that they will not make the team if they continue, and consider following through with taking away items

related, such as football boots / ball. After-all, why would they need these if they no longer play the game. Advise them that for every action, there is a consequence. In this situation, taking away the football shoes and ball are the consequence for not attending practice.

Reward motivation that leads to the accomplishment of set goals.

Ensure that rewards are only associated with motivation that is in harmony with achieving your child's set goals or will benefit humanity.

Positive Words for your child

"People often say that motivation doesn't last. Well, neither does bathing. That's why we recommend it daily"
Zig Ziglar

GUIDE → ENCOURAGE → REWARD

Francine K Woolcock

N

Nearest

& dearest

Friends:-
(Nearest & dearest)

A person known well to another and regarded with liking, affection, and loyalty;

KEEP LIKE-MINDED COMPANY

Friends are a great influence on children. Influencing what they do, what they think and believe, and ultimately, their achievements.
As parents, it is difficult to control your child's friends and trying to do so will not win you any favors.
From a young age, encourage your child to join clubs that promote positivity and success, e.g. sports clubs, humanitarian clubs (i.e. brownies & scouts), or after school tutoring in-order to meet like-minded people with similar ambitions.

BEFRIEND EXPERIENCE

Experienced people are the best sources of knowledge should your child wish to follow in the same profession or obtain a particular skill.
Encourage your child to research successful people who have what they want. Know all about that person as if they were close friends. Find out how they became successful, the obstacles they faced and how they overcame them.
Many successful people came from very humble beginnings, thus reinforcing the fact that anyone can be a success.

Positive Words for your child

"Show me your friends and I'll tell you who you are."

unknown

GUIDE ▶ **ENCOURAGE** ▶ **REWARD**

Francine K Woolcock

Optimism

Optimism:-
The tendency to expect the best and see the best in all things

It is true that your beliefs have a direct correlation with your experiences. If you believe life is great and expect great things, you will look for something positive in every situation.

This may seem a little far-fetched, because, we do experience situations which do not always produce the response that we expect, but remaining optimistic, will allow you to see a positive, even in adverse situations.

There are many universal laws that we accept yet may not understand e.g. the laws of electricity and gravity and the 'law of attraction'. Although the science behind the 'law of attraction' is not yet sound, the law claims, 'like attracts like', focusing on positivity will bring about positive experiences and focusing on negativity will bring about negative experiences. This law is accepted by several successful individuals.

Napoleon Hill once said that people who seldom succeed tend to see the hole in the donut, whilst successful people see the hole, and the donut (seeing the positive in every negative).

To encourage Optimism

If a desired result is not achieved, ensure the child is asked to state something positive from the result. This must be done without fail, at every junction where the desired result is not achieved.

Positive Words for your child

"You could say that the glass is half empty, but your Optimism tells you that the glass is also half full" adapted by Francine Woolcock

> GUIDE > ENCOURAGE > REWARD

Francine K Woolcock

Positivity

Positivity:-
Tending to emphasize what is good or laudable; constructive

THINK IT, SPEAK IT, LIVE IT

Physical health and Mental Health

The Encyclopedia of Natural Medicine states that the largest part to your overall health is from your mental health. Having positive mental health gives us the motivation to do our best that we can and are always striving to do better (Murray, Michael & Pizzorno, and Joseph: Encyclopedia of Natural Medicine (1998)(pgs. 17-19)(Revised 2nd Edition); Three River Press, New York.)

Positive mental attitude (PMA) is the philosophy that having an optimistic disposition in every situation in one's life attracts positive changes and increases achievement. It employs a state of mind that continues to seek, find and execute ways to win, or find a desirable outcome, regardless of the circumstances. It opposes negativity, defeatism and hopelessness.

REINFORCE POSITIVITY

1) Practice 'A' for 'Affirm
2) Think Happy thoughts
3) Surround yourself with positive people
4) Discourage negative self talk

Positive Words for your child

"Positive thinking will let you use the ability which you have, and that is awesome."
Zig Ziglar

GUIDE → ENCOURAGE → REWARD

What the successful teach their children –Alphabet for Success

Question

Question:-
A form of words addressed to a person in order to elicit information or evoke a response; interrogative sentence

Asking questions promotes better thinking and as a result, leads to better actions.

Excerpt from Rudyard Kipling's clever poem:

<u>Six Honest Men</u>

I have six honest serving men,
They taught me all I Know,
Their names are **What,** and **Where** and **When**
And **Why** and **How** and **Who**

'Question the Facts' game.

How to play: Ask your child a question based on a random fact. Your child must then research the answer. You then ask another question using their previous answer.

The more questions answered by your child, the more points gained. Points can be exchanged for rewards as you see fit.

Example:

Parent :   Question 1: Why is it cold?

Child: Answer 1: Because it's winter

Parent: Question 2: Why is it winter?

Child: Answer 2: Because the seasons change.

Parent: Question 3: Why do the seasons change?

This game is a great way to develop your child's inquisitive mind.

Positive Words for children

"If you don't ask the question, how do you get the answer?" Francine Woolcock

>GUIDE   >ENCOURAGE >REWARD

Francine K Woolcock

Resilience

Resilience:-

Recovering easily and quickly from shock, illness, hardship, etc

It isn't how many times you get knocked down, it's how many times you get back up that will determine your success.

The little seed knew that it had to be thrown in the dirt, covered in darkness and fight to the top to reach the light in-order to grow and blossom into a beautiful flower.

The 'Scenario' game

To encourage resilience, the scenario game forces the child to continue playing and win, or quit and loose.
You may wish to include a prize at the end to further reward the child, and motivate them to try harder.

How to play:

Step 1) Choose a scenario based on a desire or Goal.
Step 2) Add an obstacle
Step 3) The child must give you a solution to overcoming the obstacle

There are three different levels

Level 1) Introduce 3 obstacles
Level 2) Introduce 9 obstacles
Level 3) Introduce 15 obstacles

To win, the child must overcome all the obstacles in the level chosen. Choose levels in accordance with your child's ability.

If the child is unable to overcome the obstacle, they lose the game.

Example –
Goal = To get an A in science
Scenario = You need to finish your science project and hand it in tomorrow in-order to get an A .

Obstacle 1 = Oh, no, the internet has stopped working
Possible solution = Go to the library

Obstacle 2 = The library printer isn't working
Possible solution = Save the project onto a datastick

Obstacle 3 = Your datastick does not have enough memory.
Possible solution = delete some of the older files on the datastick that you no longer need.

Positive Words for children

"A Quitter never wins and a winner never quits" Napoleon Hill

GUIDE ▶ **ENCOURAGE** ▶ **REWARD**

What the successful teach their children –Alphabet for Success

Strong-minded

Decisive:-
(Strong-minded)

Characterized by the ability to make decisions, esp. quickly; resolute

Being decisive and strong-minded is not only about making quick decisions, but also about trying to make the right decisions.

Take a quick pause to think before deciding
Often bad decisions are made if the factors and outcome are not properly assessed

Better decision making comes naturally through experience and age.
Dependant on the child's age & abilities, it would be irresponsible and unrealistic to expect a child to make critical decisions for which their minds are not yet capable of analyzing. Assist children in making decisions by offering suitable choices, this way the child still feels like they are making a decision and in control and is able to build their skills for analyzing and decision making.

Experiencing the outcome of a bad decision is a crucial part of the learning process
Sometimes, the outcome following a decision is not as was expected. Allow your child to take responsibility for their decisions rather than coming to their rescue. Only then will they learn not to make that decision in the future.

To reinforce quick decision making, practice giving your children time limits in which to make the decision. These time limits must be proportional to the difficulty of the decision being made.

Positive Words for children

"The only way you can remain in control of your life is to make a decision. Do not allow others to make a decision for you, but by all means if they have experience, take their advice." Francine Woolcock

> GUIDE > ENCOURAGE > REWARD >

T

Thankful

Thankful:-
Grateful and appreciative

Give thanks and be truly happy for what you already have no-matter how much or little you have.

Thinking about what we have and associating good feelings with these thoughts, works in the same way as the 'law of attraction', the more you think of something, the more of that something you shall receive.

"A grateful mind is a great mind which eventually attracts to itself great things." –**Plato**

"What we think about and THANK about is what we bring about..." **The Secret**

LIST OF APPRECIATION
Have your child write a list of all the things they are thankful for and read that list in the morning as they wake and in the evening before sleep.

Positive Words for children

"Some people are always grumbling because roses have thorns; I am thankful that thorns have roses." Alphonse Karr

GUIDE → **ENCOURAGE** → **REWARD**

Francine K Woolcock

Unwavering

Unwavering:-

Not wavering or hesitant; resolute

KNOW YOURSELF

The first step to having an unwavering mind is to know yourself, your beliefs and your values.
With this knowledge, it is 100 times easier to stick to your decisions.

Teach your child to stand by his/ her beliefs and not to be swayed by someone else's opinion.

The 'Who am I' game.
This is a daily game in which you ask your child a question about themself. They must answer the question and record the information in a notebook. This will force the child to think about what they like, their beliefs and what type of person they are. This game is also a great game for you to learn more about your child.

Positive Words for children

"I know who I am." Francine Woolock

> GUIDE   > ENCOURAGE   > REWARD

Francine K Woolcock

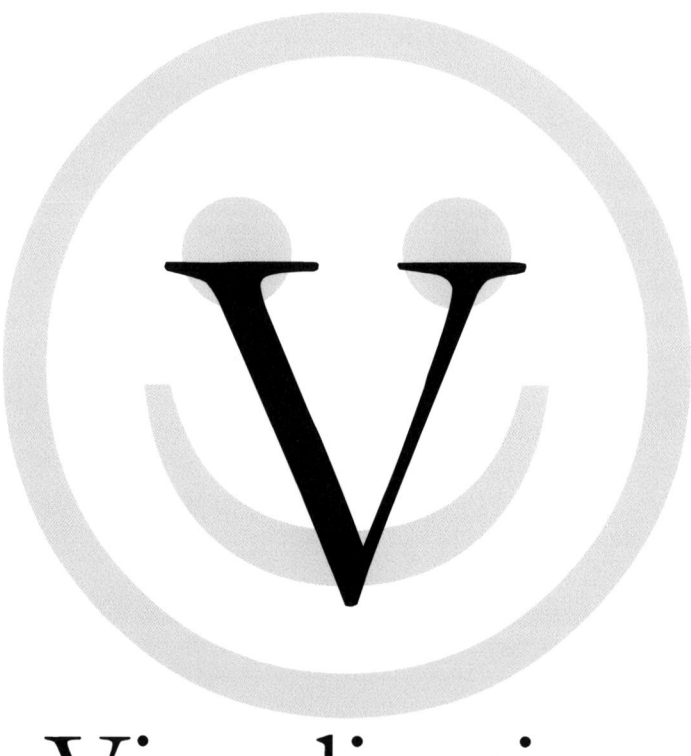

Visualization

Visualization:-

A technique involving focusing on positive mental images in order to achieve a particular goal

FROM IMAGINATION TO REALITY

Visualization is a form of conscious daydreaming whereby you imagine a situation as if it is in the present. This is a powerful technique that many athletes and successful people do daily and in some instances several times a day.

The goal is visualized over and over again until it is accepted by the higher-level subconscious mind where it works to accomplish the goal.

There is no magic involved, this is simply the power of the mind.

TEACH YOUR CHILD HOW TO VISUALISE

1) Decide on your goal and clearly define it, thinking about all the details and remain positive
2) Add emotions to your goal and add details based on the 5 senses; sight, hearing, smell, touch, taste.
3) Sit alone in a quiet place and relax. Depending on your child's age and attention span, this may be easier said than done.
4) Imagine your goal accomplished for as long as possible.

Positive Words for children

"When I was younger, I used to visualize myself scoring wonder goals, stuff like that." Wayne Rooney

GUIDE → ENCOURAGE → REWARD

Francine K Woolcock

Willpower

Willpower:-
The ability to control oneself and determine one's actions

PROOF OF THE POWER OF WILL

In a well-known experiment in the late 1960s, Psychologists Mischel and Ebbeson (1970) showed 4-year-old children a marshmallow and they told them they could have eaten one right away, or they could have had a second one if they were willing (and able) to wait for 15 min.

Mischel (1996) followed up 20 years later with the same group of children taking part in their first experiment. Surprisingly they found that those who had previously waited for 15 min had an average SAT score that was 210 points higher than those who had waited for just thirty seconds or less. Moreover, these people had more rewarding social relationship and fewer behavioral problems.

Mischel concluded that "Once you realize that willpower is just a matter of learning how to control your attention and thoughts, you can really begin to increase it." This finding has enormous implications. If willpower and self-control can be really improved and strengthened, then it is also, based on the results of this experiment, possible to improve children's future success in life.

IMPROVE A CHILD'S WILLPOWER

Willpower is like a muscle that grows stronger each time it is used. Exercise willpower and willpower will improve.
One way to do this is through delayed gratification. For younger children, try Mischel's marshmallow experiment.

Positive Words for children

"Strength does not come from physical capacity. It comes from an indomitable will." Mahatma Gandhi

GUIDE → ENCOURAGE → REWARD

Francine K Woolcock

Xenodochial

Xenodochial:-
Friendly to strangers; hospitable

Xenodochial is an adjective term derived from ancient Greek. It isn't found in the English Collins or Oxford dictionaries, however, is found in Wiktionary and Phrontistery (a dictionary for obscure words).

IT'S A SMALL WORLD
Advise children, you never know what part someone will play in your life in the future because it is indeed, a small world.

Therefore, ensure you are nice to everyone you meet and not judgmental.

ATTRACT MORE FRIENDS
Being nice to strangers will naturally attract more people to you.
Think about two people you have met, one friendly and the other not so friendly, without question, you would have been more inclined to like the person who was friendly towards you right?
The more friends your child has, the more options and connections they will have to get assistance and support in carrying out their own goals. This is not to say that all friends will have a positive influence as detailed earlier in 'Nearest & Dearest', keep like-minded company. However, the options for potential beneficial friendships will be greatly increased.

Positive Words for children

"My closest friends were once strangers". Francine Woolcock

GUIDE   ENCOURAGE   REWARD

Francine K Woolcock

Youth

Youth:-
The quality or condition of being young, immature, or inexperienced

Being young in body and mind has its advantages of time and inexperience. Give your child the best gift in life by helping them to build a strong foundation for success in the early stages of development.

RESEARCH CONDUCTED BY THE 'CENTER ON THE DEVELOPING CHILD' AT HARVARD UNIVERSITY .

http://developingchild.harvard.edu/

Experiences Build Brain Architecture
The basic architecture of the brain is constructed through a process that begins early in life and continues into adulthood. Simpler circuits come first and more complex brain circuits build on them later. Genes provide the basic blueprint, but experiences influence how or whether genes are expressed. Together, they shape the quality of brain architecture and establish either a sturdy or a fragile foundation for all of the learning, health, and behavior that follow. Plasticity, or the ability for the brain to reorganize and adapt, is greatest in the first years of life and decreases with age.

Follow this link –
http://developingchild.harvard.edu/resources/multimedia/videos/three_core_concepts/brain_architecture/

Serve & Return Interaction Shapes Brain Circuitry
One of the most essential experiences in shaping the architecture of the developing brain is "serve and return" interaction between children and significant adults in their lives. Young children naturally reach out for interaction through babbling, facial expressions, and gestures, and adults respond with the same kind of vocalizing and gesturing back at them. This back-and-forth

process is fundamental to the wiring of the brain, especially in the earliest years.

Follow this link –
http://developingchild.harvard.edu/resources/multimedia/videos/three_core_concepts/serve_and_return/

TO SUPPORT YOUR CHILD'S SUCCESS DURING THEIR DEVELOPMENT, FOLLOW THESE 5 STEPS
1) Practice regular Interaction
2) Introduce them to new experiences
3) Correct negative / harmful practices before they develop into habits.
4) Regularly assess your child's development
5) Guide, Encourage and Reward.

Positive Words for children

"Good habits formed at youth make all the difference."
Aristotle

GUIDE ENCOURAGE REWARD

What the successful teach their children –Alphabet for Success

Z

Zest

Zest:-
Invigorating or keen excitement or enjoyment

The odds of being born are not accurately known however, there have been various numbers such as 1 in 4,000,00 and even 1 in 400 trillion.

We can therefore conclude that, to be alive is a miracle.

A LITTLE MIRACLE MESSAGE FOR YOUR CHILD

There is only one you and there will never be another you. You have something that only you can give to the world, try to find your purpose, your special gift, and share it with the world.

Words of Wisdom

"Have a Zest for life and life will provide you with Zest."
Francine Woolcock

GUIDE ENCOURAGE REWARD

References

A-Z Characteristic meanings taken from The Collins English Dictionary, online, <http://www.collinsdictionary.com/>Accessed 26th December 2013

Article, 'Willpower in children and adults: a survey of results and economic implications', <http://link.springer.com/article/10.1007/s12232-010-0103-8/fulltext.html> accessed 26th December 2013

Online site, unusual words- Phrontistery xenodochial,<http://phrontistery.info>accessed 26th December 2013

Quotes from-

Notable Quotes
www.notable-quotes.com

Brainy Quote
www.brainyquote.com

ABOUT THE AUTHOR

The Author Francine Kaydian Woolcock was born in Kingston Jamaica and emigrated to the UK aged 8.
Always a high achiever and with a range of talents, Francine found it difficult to stick to one interest being the jack of all trades but master of none.
Incorporated and dissolved a catering company at the age of 19, graduated from Kings College University with a degree in Computer Science aged 22, however, pursued a career in Facility Management aged 25.

In the year 2013, seeing family members struggle and desperately wanting to help her siblings succeed, Francine made a definite decision to become successful.
At the age of 27 she began conducting extensive research on the successful and how they acquired their success, what made them different and why they could acquire success whilst others struggled to find purpose and happiness.
Why was this information not common knowledge? And if it was common knowledge, why was it not more widely practiced?

This has led her to the attributes of success mentioned in this book.

Finally a passion that she has truly fallen in-love with.

Printed in Great Britain
by Amazon